# South Dakota 100

**FIRST EDITION**

Copyright © 1988 J & J Publishing Company
Box 170 R.R. #1
Canton, South Dakota 57013

J & J Publishing Company
Box 170 R.R. #1
Canton, South Dakota 57013

Library of Congress Catalog Card Number: 88-82023

ISBN: 0-937959-51-0

# South Dakota 100

## Strasser/Townsend/Woster

1889 · 1989
South Dakota

A Centennial Project of the KELO-LAND TV Stations

J & J Publishing Company
Box 170 R.R. #1
Canton, South Dakota 57013

The KELO-LAND Gold Rush of 1961 was the climax of the Dakota Territory Centennial Celebration in South Dakota. More than 150,000 people attended the two-day event in which Manchester, a normally sleepy town of 81 population, became the largest city in five states for one week-end.

Attractions included a carnival, camporee, talent show, square dances, fireworks, and celebrity guest appearances. It was climaxed by the actual Gold Rush in which 1439 people who had won gold shovels during the summer dug in a special plot for $35,000 in prizes.

Lawrence Welk, Clint Eastwood, Joe Feeney, Yogi Bear, Cindy Bear, Huckleberry Hound, Captain Eleven, Governor Gubbrud, Senators Karl Mundt and Francis Case, and Representative Ben Reifel joined numerous other dignitaries in digging for an additional $3500 in prizes for various charitable organizations.

In preparation for the Gold Rush, honorary gold shovels were presented to dozens of officials including President John F. Kennedy, the President of Mexico, and the King of Norway.

A historical marker was erected at the site of the Gold Rush to commemorate this unique Dakota Territory Centennial event.

Joel Strasser    Terry Woster    Jack Townsend

All three people involved in the creation of South Dakota 100 are South Dakota natives. They share a special love for the state and its people.

**Joel Strasser** was born in Fairview. He attended Augustana College and the Progressive School of Photography in New Haven, Connecticut. He served four years in the U.S. Air Force.

Since 1958 Joel has been self-employed as a photographer specializing in commercial and architectural work and photographic art. He has received national recognition including the Silver Medal of Photography from the American Advertising Federation. He holds the degrees of Master of Photography and Photographic Craftsman.

Joel is a member of Cameracraftsmen of America, American Society of Photographers, and Professional Photographers of America.

In 1984 he published *Where My Heart Is,* a book about his life in South Dakota.

Joel and wife Lavonne have three sons: Jeff, Jay, and Joel Z.

**Terry Woster** was born and raised on a farm north of Reliance in central South Dakota. He majored in journalism at South Dakota State University and has been in newspaper work for the past 20 years.

After two years in the Sports Department of the *Sioux Falls Argus Leader,* he served as Associated Press correspondent in Pierre. After a stint at the *Pierre Capital Journal* he began his present job as Pierre correspondent for the *Argus Leader.*

Terry's wife Nancy is a native of Chamberlain. They have three children: Jennifer, Scott and Andy.

Terry finds the people of South Dakota fascinating. This is reflected in the column he writes for the *Argus Leader* which features warm and human sketches of his life in the state and the people he has met along the way.

**Jack Townsend** was born in Sioux Falls. He attended Augustana College and the University of Missouri School of Journalism, returning later to the University of South Dakota for an MBA.

After service in the U.S. Army, he joined KELO-TV in 1954, during the first year of television operation. After fourteen years as Promotion Director and Operations Manager, he moved to the Sales Department where he now serves as KELO-LAND TV Sales Manager.

Jack and his wife Patricia have six children: John, Mary, Mike, Jim, Bill and Dave.

# South Dakota Seasons

South Dakota is a state of remarkable seasons and remarkable people. The seasons are remarkable for their breathtaking change from a bone-chilling December's night blizzard to the soul-scorching blast furnace of a wheat-harvest July afternoon. The people are remarkable for their ability to adapt to those wild swings in climate. South Dakotans, both the ones who were born and raised here and the ones who came to the state later and made it their home, have learned not just to endure the harsh winters and dry summers but to embrace them, reveling in the specialness of each season, loving its unique qualities.

Anyone who has stood at the top of Iron Mountain and watched a late-April sunset in the Black Hills, who has drifted in a sailboat over the rippled mirror of Lake Oahe in July, who has scuffed through red and brown leaves near Sand Lake in October or who has watched the sun sparkle against the frozen falls of the Sioux River understands how distinct South Dakota's seasons are and appreciates how each season has affected the way they look at life and their world.

# SPRING

Spring teases its way into South Dakota each year, and South Dakotans are ready for it long before it decides to settle in and stay.

Spring comes for a tantalizing day or two in late February, rushing the season with a sudden surge of sunshine and a 70-degree day or two that make the snowdrifts shrink and run into the gulleys and down the gutters. Just as suddenly, it's gone, dashing away ahead of a bitter northwest wind that howls in from Montana or Wyoming. The passing winter isn't ready yet to give up its frigid grip on the plains.

Spring returns early in March, offering little hints of what's to come later in the season. There's a mellow breeze that tickles the back of the neck, the merest glimpse of a new bud on a bare tree branch, the promise of warm sunshine just beyond the next, maybe last, wet snowstorm whirling out of the Rocky Mountains. Perhaps because the fading winter has been so fierce, there's a warm fullness to these early spring days, a feeling much like the one that comes with the visit of a distant but much-loved cousin making her annual trip to the old family home.

Ranchers in five-buckled overshoes kick through the melting snow that huddles like old pillows in the still-brown grass of their pastures. They use an old gunny sack to wipe down a shivering calf born far too soon, and they study the curly red hide and white face as the youngster nuzzles its mother for milk.

Farm children love these early spring days when the new calves are coming and their fathers are wondering whether the next storm will be too much for the young animals. There's always a chance that Dad will show up at the back door with one of the critters cradled in his big arms. When that happens, the excited children fight to see who gets to feed the calf from a bottle as it lies on soft wool blankets in a corner of the back porch.

The lucky one holds tightly with both hands while the other children crowd close and giggle at the calf's bright pink tongue stretching for the bottle.

On clear spring days, farmers gun their four-wheel-drive jeeps through the deep puddles of water in rutted tracks along the edges of the wheat fields. They pull into the winter wheat and park on a high spot where it's dry. They step out and kneel in the damp soil, surveying the tiny stalks of green wheat just beginning to come to life again after the dormant winter, and they wonder about the chances for a good, soaking rain in the next couple of weeks to spur the sluggish crop to early growth.

In towns across the state, jump ropes are out and whirling along the sidewalks. After school the boys dash home to grab their scarred fielder's mitts and scuffed baseballs and head for the park for a game of 500 or work-

up or one of the half-dozen other pick-up games small town boys learn early.

In the yards and gardens, South Dakotans are busy, too, raking away the winter's accumulation of soggy leaves and small sticks, preparing the soil for the tomatoes and beans and squash. Many of them, although it's really not warm enough yet — especially when the sun goes under the huge, white clouds that float low in the sky — work in short-sleeved shirts and shorts, shivering when they're in the shade under the trees but smiling to themselves when the direct sunlight soaks into their shoulders.

Spring in South Dakota is a time of remarkable hope and faith. South Dakota believes what its people do will bear fruit, whether it's in the grain fields, the pastures or the playgrounds.

Like one of grandma's soft, warm quilts, hope spreads across the land when spring comes to the prairie.

Sunshine and ice combine to decorate South Dakota for spring.

Farm families greet spring with one eye on the sky. Change is the only dependable ingredient of South Dakota spring weather.

Oh, every year hath its winter,
  And every year hath its rain —
But a day is always coming
  When the birds go north again.
          *Ella Higginson*

South Dakota's state flower is one of the first to appear on the prairie. A member of the buttercup family, the Pasqueflower blooms as early as March, often before the surrounding vegetation turns green. These were captured near Wessington Springs.

Bloodroot and Trillium are harbingers of spring.
These were found in woodlands near Canton.

Newton Hills State Park in southeastern
South Dakota is a popular spot to
welcome spring.

Delicate fresh green
aspen trees grace
Harney Peak Valley in
the Black Hills.

Bloodroot is named for its red roots and sap.

Slim Buttes in Harding County is a little-known
beauty spot. It is in Custer National Forest, west
of Reva. The Battle of Slim Buttes was fought
there in 1876.

A cornfield near Chester proves
irresistible to a flock of spring
visitors.

This resident of McCrossan Boys Ranch
greets spring with a smile.

All the signs of spring are not welcome. Bugs embrace a cedar tree at Fairview.

Early residents promoted the falls of the Sioux River as a power source for the Queen Bee Flour Mill. Today the falls serve only as a beauty spot in one of the many Sioux Falls parks.

The Delbridge
Museum of
Natural History
contains a world
class collection of
stuffed animals,
the result of a
lifetime of big
game hunting by
Henry
Brockhouse.

Relics of pre-historic creatures provide a fascinating and educational walk for visitors to Fossil Trail in the Badlands.

Years of wind and weather have left their mark on a barn door in central South Dakota.

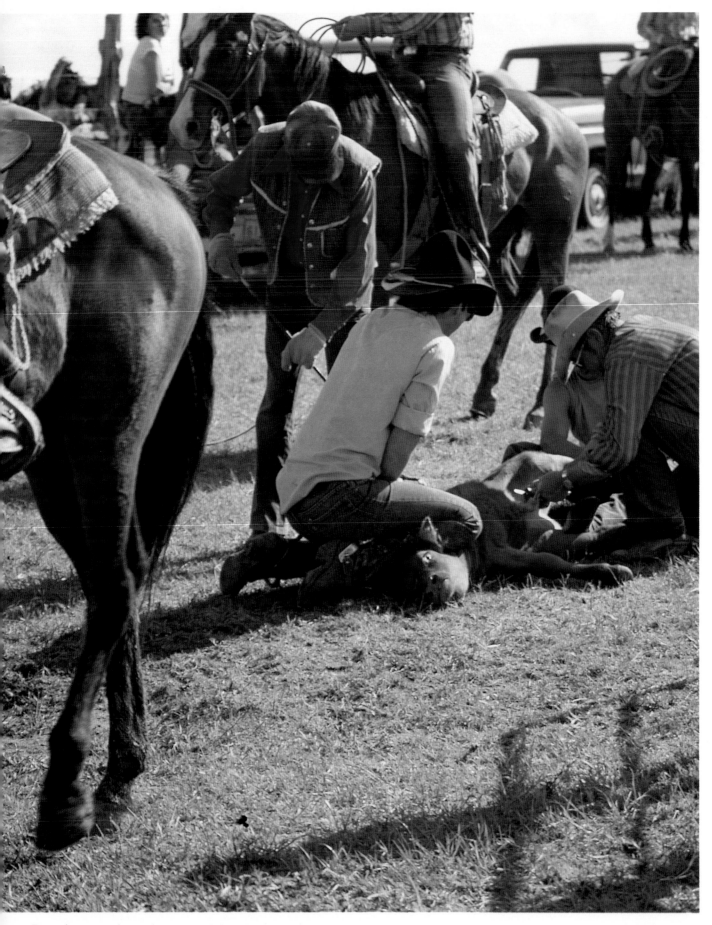

Ranchers and cowboys at White River brand calves much as
they did 100 years ago.

Main stem dams have created a haven for wildlife along
the Missouri River. This scene is at Lake Andes.

If you are a fisherman spring means just one thing. This one tries his luck above Rough Lock Falls in the Black Hills.

Reeds form a pattern in the water near Webster.

"Hands on" is the motto of the petting section
at the Great Plains Zoo in Sioux Falls.

In appreciation of the important role honey plays in our state's
economy, the honey bee was named state insect in 1978.

Black Hills National Cemetery
"These heroes are dead. They died for liberty—they died for us. They are at rest. They sleep in the land they made free, under the flag they rendered stainless, under the solemn pines, the sad hemlocks, the tearful willows, the embracing vines."
**_Robert Green Ingersoll_**

A South Dakota mother and child represent the eternal verities of life. Spring is the perfect season for Mothers Day. . .the time to celebrate birth, nurturing, and new beginnings.

A wooden fence at Stamford frames the old railroad station.

Black Hills National Forest includes many scenes of spectacular beauty including Horseshoe Lake near Mount Rushmore.

# SUMMER

South Dakota has summer days when the sun bakes down so hard that even the south wind refuses to stir and people gasp for breath as they fight through the almost physical barrier of heat toward the air-conditioned office or home. The evening weatherman tells his television audience, "There isn't any relief in sight," and entire families groan, knowing the scorching days will stretch through another week.

When a hot spell has the plains wrapped like an electric blanket on high, people retreat to their homes, keeping window shades pulled down tight and air conditioners whining through the night. On evenings like this, the few who venture out for a walk through the neighborhood — either because they're less susceptible to heat or because they don't have central air or a window cooling unit — find the town silent, but for the hum of cooling fans and heat exchangers. They walk past dark houses and empty yards, trying to move as little as possible, looking for a chance to cool for a moment in the mist of a lawn sprinkler.

When a hot spell is on the state, the grown-ups sit close to the fan and tell the younger ones about the days before air conditioning. It was a different world, they'll say, and looking back, we're not sure how we stood up under it. Guess we just didn't know it could be any other way so we suffered along with everybody else, they'll say.

Of course the hot spells don't last forever, it just seems that way when they're baking the lawns and corn and second crop of alfalfa. Most of South Dakota's summer is a pleasing time.

The summer starts with a series of cloudy, drizzling down days and overcast nights that put a luxurious green into the blades of grass and push the leaves out full on elm and ash and oak trees. Gradually, the clouds thin out and the rains come less frequently. The storms are spectacular during these days and nights — wild displays of murderous lightning and crashing thunder that sweep over the countryside atop towering menacing black clouds. Harvesters in the wheat fields watch the western horizon as the thunderheads build, and they push their combines and trucks to the limit, trying to get the last bushels of grain cut and hauled off to the elevator in town before the skies open and pour water into the stubble fields.

Along about the end of July, the rain stops for good in the western part of South Dakota. The clouds continue to build in the west each afternoon, thunder and lightning crackle like dry leaves under a herd of deer, but no moisture falls. Day after day it happens, until, finally, the clouds themselves give up and just don't show up one day. For dry-land farmers, the dog days are on the land, and they squint into the dusty distance and wonder if the milo and corn has enough growth on it and enough moisture left in the subsoil to make it through until cutting time.

For all the worry late summer brings to the farm families, it's a time of special treats for weekend fishermen and pleasure boaters, as well as for the softball teams that gather at diamonds every evening to challenge each other's skill and stretch the day into late evening's shadows. The very sameness of every day in this time of the year makes for flat waters on the lakes and clear skies for the ballplayers. A drive on one of the state's secondary highways will carry you past small town after small town with a fenced off ball diamond cut into the corner of some pasture just at the edge of the village. For visitors from other states, the sight of a trio of light towers rising out of the prairie grass at the edge of a town that's just a dot on their map is always surprising. Who'd have thought there was organized athletics clear out here?

South Dakota's summers test the mettle of the state's citizens, but few fail to pass the test. The state is peopled by hardy stock, and they seem unimpressed to think that in the space of only six months they can go from enduring nights with temperatures as low as 30 degrees below zero and more to days when the mercury tops out at 115 degrees above zero, sometimes higher in the real scorchers. Tourists shake their heads and wonder at the people who live here. South Dakotans mop their brows, shrug their shoulders and get to work. They know fall is on its way.

The world's only Corn Palace is located in Mitchell. Built in 1892, its decorations of corn, grain and natural grasses are changed every year.

All that remains of Fort Randall on the Missouri River near
Lake Andes are these ruins of the post chapel. Fort Randall was once
the main U.S. Army post in the Dakotas.

A familiar sight in the 20's and 30's, family-owned gasoline stations gave way to chain-operated and franchised service stations in the 40's and 50's. Many are now closed or turned into convenience stores. Feay's Garage in Sioux Falls was one of the last to go.

The bubble-gum chewing donkey at the Great Plains Zoo is always good for a laugh.

Mourners in Lennox bury a loved one.

This Independence Day scene in Canton
might have been taken in almost any
South Dakota town on July Fourth.

The original settlers of Sioux Falls were chased away by Indians. But they returned and in 1857 became the first white town in South Dakota.

Pierre became the capital on November 2, 1889 when South Dakota was admitted to the union.

The Needles can be seen as the background for beautiful
Stockade Lake in the Black Hills.

Mark Twain had his opinion of golf. He
called it "A good walk . . . spoiled".

"A blade of grass is always a blade of grass,
whether in one country or another."
*Samuel Johnson*

My heart leaps up when I behold
A rainbow in the sky:
So was it when my life began;
So is it now I am a man.
*William Wordsworth*

Invisible beauty has a word so brief
A flower can say it or a shaken leaf,
But few may ever snare it in a song.
    *Grace Hazard Conkling*

Sculptor Steve Thomas created "Sea
Dream" from steel plates welded together.
A representation of ocean spray beating
against rocks, it was placed at the corner
of 10th Street and Second Avenue in
Sioux Falls in 1985.

Sunset over a farm near Brookings.

The wisdom of the ages is in the eyes
of a woman watching her family in the
park at Lennox.

Unheralded beauty in the blossom
of an alfalfa plant near Meckling.

Innumerable as the stars of night,
Or stars of morning, dewdrops which the sun
Impearls on every leaf and every flower.
*John Milton*

Billy Graham brings his Crusade for Christ to
Howard Wood Field in Sioux Falls.

Every cloud engenders not a storm.
*William Shakespeare*

Heading for home after a full day of boating
on Lewis and Clark Lake.

What is better on a summer day than
sitting around talking things over?

Boy comes face to face with nature at
Oakwood Lakes near Bruce.

A Burlington Northern freight train
disappears over the prairie horizon at Ipswich.

Travelers on Interstate 90 are treated to a
beautiful panorama of the Missouri River
as they cross it at Chamberlain.

The Shrine of Democracy at Mount
Rushmore attracts two million visitors
annually. Sculptor Gutzon Borglum
devoted fourteen years to this
monumental project.

The Black Hills really should have been named mountains. They are
the highest mountain range between the Rockies and the Alps.
Harney Peak towers 7242 feet above sea level.

In South Dakota the family is still the basic unit which holds
society together. This farm family is from Howard.

In earlier days competition was keen to determine whose team of
horses could outpull the challengers. Today in Fairview the
principle is the same, but the pulling is done by tractors.
The competition is still fierce.

When Dakota Territory was ready for admission to the Union, both states wanted the name Dakota because of the world-wide reputation of "Dakota No. 1 Hard Wheat". Dakota wheat such as this field near Redfield is still the finest in the world.

Water has always been of primary importance to South Dakota.
Whether it is in a pool at Chamberlain for a summer swim,
generating power as seen here at the Oahe Dam Powerhouse above
Pierre, or just raining on the crops, nobody takes it for granted.

Prairie Skyscrapers.

A man does not plant a tree for himself, he
plants it for posterity.
*Alexander Smith*

A windmill stands watch over an
abandoned farmstead.

OATS—A grain which in England is
generally given to horses, but in Scotland
supports the people.
*Samuel Johnson*

This contoured cornfield near Fairview is typical of the rich farmland of southeastern South Dakota.

The Sioux Falls Stockyards is a giant hotel for livestock. All species of livestock are bought and sold by private treaty and auction. Since 1981 it has been number one in the nation in total receipts.

85

One of the little-known facts about South Dakota is that the sunsets are the most beautiful in the world. Here is a good example, captured at Aurora.

Additional evidence from southeastern South Dakota.

Life-size re-creations of pre-historic dinosaurs modeled in cement overlook Rapid City in Dinosaur Park. The reptiles inhabited the Black Hills area forty million years ago during the Mesozoic era.

Needles Highway is one of the finest scenic drives in the United States. Twenty miles of hairpin curves wind around breathtaking views of granite spires and snake through three narrow tunnels.

In South Dakota, the road stretches straight as an arrow, as far as the eye can see, almost to tomorrow.

An instinctive taste teaches men to build their churches in flat
countries with spire steeples, which as they cannot be referred to any
other object, point as with silent finger to the sky and stars.
    *Samuel Taylor Coleridge*

I pledge allegiance to the flag of the United States, and to
the republic for which it stands . . .

The best place to grow watermelon is in sandy soil. The best place to eat watermelon is anywhere. This feast is taking place at the Lewis and Clark Boy Scout Camp near Tabor.

South Dakota boasts several fine medical centers including this one at Sioux Valley Hospital in Sioux Falls.

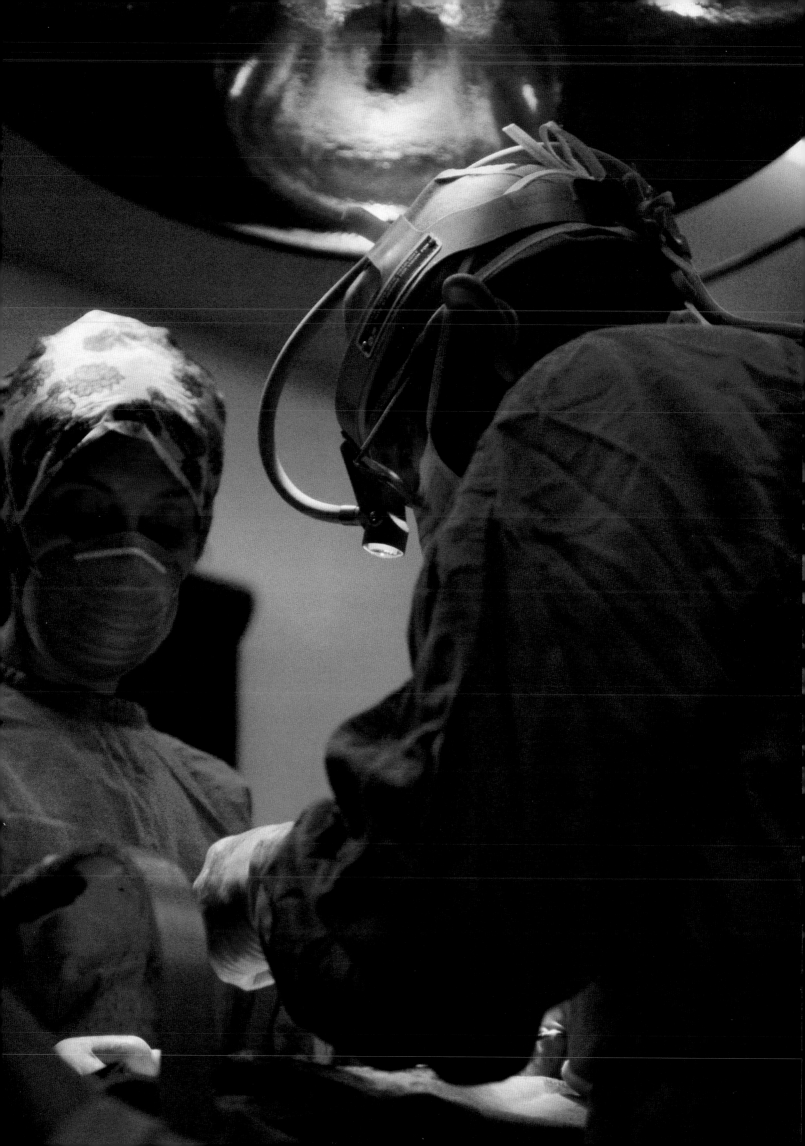

Lake Francis Case was formed by Fort
Randall Dam which was completed in
1952. It has 540 miles of shoreline,
stretching from Lake Andes to above
Chamberlain.

Big Stone Lake on the Minnesota border
at Milbank was named for the granite
outcroppings nearby. Hunter, royal purple
and mahogany granite are quarried here
and sent all over the country, primarily
for use in tombstones.

Wheat field north of Watertown.

The fog comes on little cat feet.
*Carl Sandburg*

Worm or beetle—drought or tempest
 —on a farmer's land may fall,
Each is loaded full o' ruin,
but a mortgage beats 'em all.
    *Will Carleton*

No enemy
But winter and rough weather.
    *William Shakespeare*

Southeastern South Dakota is the home of many fertile
and productive farms.

Horses graze in the cool, lush beauty of Beaver Creek.

Cattle graze in the fog near Harrisburg.

This mite perched on a weed provides a
pleasing pattern of light and texture at
Sisseton.

The church at Wounded Knee in Shannon County marks the
National Historical Site of the Wounded Knee Massacre. On
December 29, 1890, 84 Indian men and boys, 44 women, and 18
children were killed. It was the last significant battle between the
plains Indians and the U.S. Army.

A resident of Wounded Knee looks out the door
of her home on the Pine Ridge Reservation.

A windmill stands lonely sentinel on the prairie at Polo.

In the rangeland around Platte, everyone is
directly or indirectly involved with cattle.

Deadwood retains much of the old west flavor from its wide open past. It was the home of many colorful and unsavory characters such as gold miners, gamblers, and the likes of Wild Bill Hickok and Calamity Jane.

The Badlands are the result of 25 million years of erosion by wind and water. The spectacular result was named in the 1700's by French Canadian fur trappers who called them "bad lands to travel across".

The Big Sioux River winds its way through
eastern South Dakota starting in Grant
County. Below Sioux Falls it forms the Iowa
border until it empties into the Missouri River
at Sioux City.

Another spectacular South Dakota
sunset in the making.

Grass in the front yard of a home in
Aberdeen reveals unexpected beauty in
the dew of morning.

These ugly ducklings grew up to be
swans in Sioux Falls.

# FALL

If you polled South Dakotans about which season is their favorite, chances are autumn would come out on top. Fall in South Dakota is a magical time, a season of soft colors and warm days that make the students hurrying across campus, the farmers cutting fragrant silage and the factory worker reporting for the morning shift forget that the lengthening shadows and chilly nights mean winter is coming next.

In fact, the splashes of bright leaves in golds and reds, and the crisp air that somehow feels cleaner than any other time of the year, make it easy to think the days are growing longer, when just the opposite is happening. Autumn began, really, when the sun began to slip lower in the sky each day, way back before summer really got hot.

Fall is a time of gathering, all across South Dakota. The ranchers use pressure from their knees and a gentle hand on the leather reins to coax cowponies down dry-grass draws to bring the hereford and angus cows and calves up from the summer pastures and closer to the home place, where stacks of gray-brown hay or soaring bundles of bales wait to feed the herds through the winter. Before the cold weather really hits, many cattlemen will be branding, and hardly a farm boy ever grew up in South Dakota who can't feel the nip of an early October morning without recalling the pungent odor of scorched hair and the plaintive bawl of a new-branded calf trotting away from the chute in search of its mother.

Fall in South Dakota is when folks in town dig into the bottom drawers for their sweaters, knowing that by mid-day, they'll have shed the extra layer, rolled up their shirt sleeves and perspired freely as they worked in the yard, clearing away the dead vines and crackling stalks of last summer's garden. Fall is Saturday mornings when it seems every resident in the neighborhood is out on the front lawn, raking the thick piles of leaves or leaning on the rake and sipping steaming coffee while a next-door buddy complains about the leaves blowing into his yard. And it's a time when anyone who ever grew up in a small town remembers the sharp sweetness of burning leaves raked into the concrete at the curb and set afire while the adults stood around to talk and make sure the light breeze didn't carry the flames onto the dormant lawn.

And fall, perhaps more than any other season, is memories. The memories are sharper, more lasting, maybe because the days are so soft and the colors so clear. Weddings may take place in June, but who hasn't kept at least one sweet memory of an October romance, of a victory dance after the homecoming football game on Friday night, or a walk, hand-in-hand, across campus on Sunday afternoon. And, for those fortunate enough to have shared a kiss, with fallen leaves whispering along the ground and the afternoon sunlight winking through the tree branches, nothing that follows will ever quite measure up to that moment.

November is a transition, a bridge from the summer to coming winter, and even though there's almost always at least one vicious snowstorm, fall takes one last fling. It's a rare season when Thanksgiving afternoon doesn't include at least a half-hearted game of touch football after the big dinner, and the players find that their jackets are just too much. They toss them carelessly onto porches and play with fierce abandon, getting in the last forward passes and off-tackle dives of the season, then sprawling tired and satisfied in the grass and debating the chances that there'll be an early snowfall in December to give a base for Black Hills skiing.

Fall in South Dakota is all those things, and this, too: An unsettling restlessness that gnaws at the pit of the stomach when darkness comes before the supper hour is finished late in the season. The season is ending, and even South Dakotans who embrace the sudden harshness of winter's first real storm seem reluctant to let the mellow autumn slip away for another year.

Slip away it does, though, and sometime in December, the sun slants low and cold, not the soft September sun at all but a hard, bitter light, at once bright but distant. There's an edge to the wind that wasn't there last week, and South Dakotans unconsciously pull their jacket collars close as they hurry from house to garage or from store to store.

The dalliance with fall is amost over, and it's time to prepare, physically and mentally, for the struggle that a new winter brings.

Wildflowers abound throughout the
state. Late spring and late summer
offer the best variety of prairie
flowers, but many species are at their
best in early spring and autumn.

Rapid City's "Stavkirke" is an exact
replica of the famous 800-year old
Borgund Church in Norway.

In late August, Prairie Village at Madison
is host to the annual Prairie Village
Steam Threshing Jamboree where antique
farm machinery performs just as it did in
the 1890's.

Sioux Falls offers cyclists more than
12 miles of bike trails, mostly along
the Big Sioux River.

South Dakota provides a vital part of our nation's defense. Ellsworth Air Force Base is home for the B-1 Bomber. Missile sites are scattered throughout the western part of the state.

Twenty-five million years ago, the now desolate Badlands area between the White and Cheyenne rivers was a lush home for prehistoric creatures. Today only a few hardy animals are able to survive in this stark, dry wasteland.

The statue of Moses on the campus of Augustana College is an authorized reproduction of the original by Michelangelo. It was a gift of Sioux Falls native industrialist Thomas Fawick to the college.

Ben Black Elk at his home in Manderson. For more than 25 years Ben posed for pictures dressed in his native attire at Mount Rushmore.

Lake Lakota is a 90-acre lake created by damming
Patee Creek at Newton Hills State Park.

The Monarch butterfly is sometimes called the
Milkweed butterfly because its larvae feed on
the leaves of the milkweed plant.

131

Light fog provides a translucent veil
for the pines and aspens of Black
Hills National Forest.

The milkweed takes its name from the milky
juice or latex it secretes.

Fall is particularly colorful in the 73,000 acres of Custer State Park located in the southwestern corner of the state.

The southeastern corner has its own fall beauty. This lovely stretch of the Big Sioux River is at Jefferson.

One of the best ways to enjoy Newton
Hills State Park is on horseback on the
excellent bridle trails.

For still the ancient riddles mar
Our joy in man, in leaf, in star.
The Whence and Whither give no rest,
The Wherefore is a hopeless quest.
*Sir William Watson*

Love all God's creation, the whole and every grain of sand in it. Love every leaf, every ray of God's light. Love the animals, love the plants, love everything. If you love everything, you will perceive the divine mystery in things. Once you perceive it, you will begin to comprehend it better every day. And you will come at last to love the whole world with an all embracing love.

*Fyodor Dostoyevsky*

Everybody likes a parade. This one is
celebrating homecoming in Canton.

Stringing beads can be very serious business.

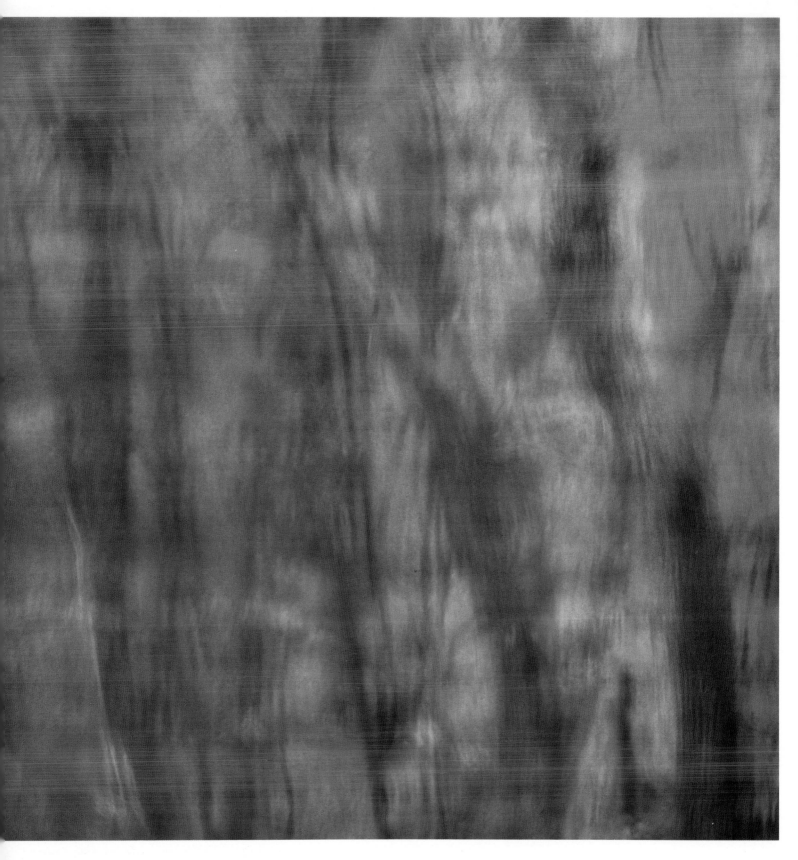

Rain falls in the woods, and it has a
misty dreamlike quality. The drops fall to
the ground and disappear. The sound is
soft and gentle, a murmur of approval.

The rain stops and the sun returns.
A million diamonds sparkle in its
light. A yellow leaf becomes a work
of art. The forest is renewed.

When tillage begins, other arts follow. The farmers
therefore are the founders of human civilization.
  *Daniel Webster*

Mata Paha or Bear Butte stands in solitary splendor on the plains east of Sturgis. It is a holy mountain for the Sioux and Cheyenne Indians.

Introduced to the state in 1898, the Chinese
Ringneck Pheasant has provided prime
hunting for many residents and visitors. It is
the state bird of South Dakota.

Autumn lights a fire of sumac across the state.

The quackgrass stands in gentle
profusion, waiting for winter's snow.

At Lake Lakota even the weeds are
pretty if you look at them in a
happy frame of mind.

151

Two churches and two
horses at Rosebud.

Some walk for exercise. Some walk for
pleasure. And some walk because it is the
best way to get where they want to be.

South Dakota sunrises aren't bad either.
This one is at Elk Point.

I believe a leaf of grass is no less than the
journey-work of the stars.
    *Walt Whitman*

A silent cry for help is unheard as an
ancient barn sinks quietly into oblivion.

As a hummingbird flies full speed
through the oak forest, this is the
view it sees. (We think.)

Heap high the farmer's wintry hoard!
 Heap high the golden corn!
No richer gift has Autumn poured
 From out her lavish horn!
*John Greenleaf Whittier*

# WINTER

South Dakota's winters are so ferocious sometimes that they instill a special pride in the people who live through them. There's a sense of competition sometimes, almost like the school boys challenging one another over who's big brother is toughest. People in Watertown and Aberdeen and Mobridge and Lemmon may shiver under the onslaught of an old-fashioned blizzard, but just try to tell them that some other state, or some other town in South Dakota, had it worse this time. They'll leap to their feet to tell you how things really were here, and if that's not quite enough, they'll take you back to the winter of 1950 or 1962 or 1968 and tell you how many days the wind blew without let-up or how high the drifts piled on the north side of the barn. South Dakotans complain a lot about the weather, winter more than any

other season. Yet they wouldn't know how to live if all the seasons were the same, if the climate never changed and the snow never danced crazily on the strength of a howling wind.

Winter in South Dakota is a time to be indoors whenever possible. The sports go inside, to overheated, stuffy gymnasiums where young men and women in shorts dribble and pass and shoot a basketball with one eye on the game clock and the other on the tournament season that starts in late February. Noisy, perspiring fans holler and clap, slap the players on the backs and pause at the door to the oustide, hesitating just a second as the sub-zero temperature chills the moisture on their foreheads.

Only the young and the working people are outside when winter wraps South Dakota in its coldest grip each year. Mothers stuff young children into sweaters and jackets and snowsuits and mittens and shiver as they watch their boys and girls waddle across the driveway and plunge face first into the deepest snowbank in the neighborhood. When finally they call the youngsters in, the faces are shining red with cold, the fingers barely move but the open-mouthed grins don't waver for an instant. The young love South Dakota's winters.

In the country, the feeling is less love than grudging respect. In spite of all the modern machinery and new methods, the men and women who farm and ranch the prairie still must do many winter things the way their parents and grandparents did before them. There's only one way to be sure the cattle have water, and that's to take an axe and smash through the thick ice covering the stock dams. The chips of ice fly through the air and land spinning, to skid along the frozen pond. The cattle, thirsty and cold, paw the snow and snort, sending huge clouds of gray steam into the bitter air as the farmer swings again and again at the ice. There's no way to handle that job without coming away soaked to the knees, just as there'e not way to haul hay down to the pasture without leaving the shelter of the tractor cab to fumble with numb fingers at the stubborn gate latch.

If the young love winter, the farmers and ranchers survive it, and in surviving, respect it. Live in this country long enough and you're sure to run into someone with a personal story of how he took one chance too many on a snowy night and wound up stuck in a drifted ditch, alone and cold and frightened. The newest cars, the most powerful four-wheel-drive pickups and the most expensive highways don't mean a thing when the temperature drops to 20 degrees below zero and the wind is throwing snow through the sky so that the headlights don't even pick up the reflectorized markers at the edge of the roadway.

The harsh days and nights of South Dakota's winters are as severe as any you'll find anywhere. But the mild days — ah, they make up for everything. They come on their own schedule, but predictably sometime in late January, again in the middle of February and for a longer stay in March, these good days of winter. The wind is silent, the sky is so blue and cloudless it almost looks like a plastic dome circling the earth. The frozen fields are covered with snow that glistens like spilled sugar in the sunlight. At night, the full moon is high and cold and as pale as butter, a tiny hole in the purple sky. The air tingles as it goes into the lungs, and the snow crackles under bootheels. Winter days and nights like that can make you almost believe that time is standing still.

Time doesn't stand still, of course. Each sub-zero day, each wind-chill announcement and each new snowfall brings spring, that old tease, one day closer.

South Dakotans are ready for spring before it arrives, but more than a few of them feel a sense of loss at the departing winter, whether they'd admit it or not. It's a remarkable time of year, and it has it's special place for the people of this remarkable state.

A pine tree stands so lonely
In the North where the high winds blow,
He sleeps; and the whitest blanket
Wraps him in ice and snow.
*Heinrich Heine*

While the earth remaineth, seedtime and harvest, and cold and heat, and summer and winter, and day and night shall not cease.
*Genesis. VIII, 22*

Winter shows its varied beauty in these scenes from the two
southern corners of the state. Custer Peak forms a background
for the pine-fringed meadow at the left. Newton Hills in
southeastern South Dakota provides a tableau of barren limbs
and snow in the picture above.

169

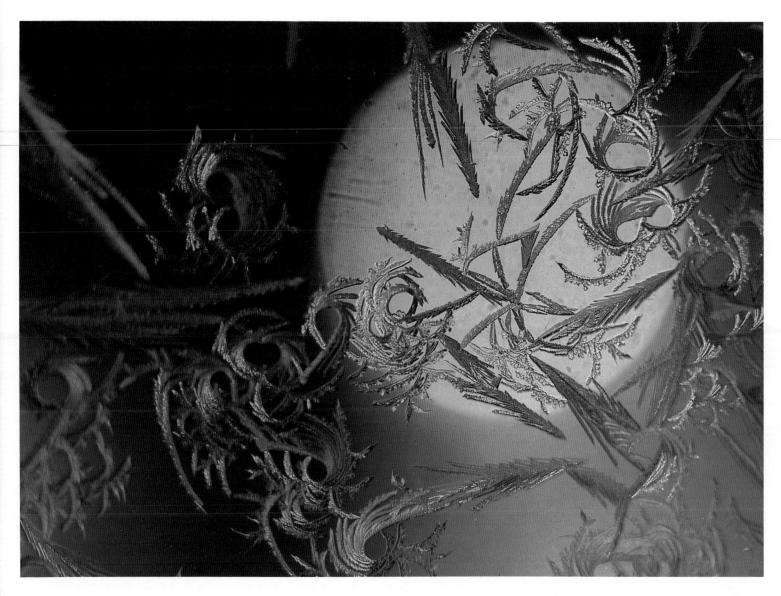

Late afternoon sun forms a surrealistic
still life with frost on the window.

A lone tree stands sentinel on a winter
road in Lincoln County.

173

Now the North wind ceases,
The warm South-west awakes,
The heavens are out in fleeces,
And earth's green banner shakes.
*George Meredith*

For winter's rains and ruins are over,
And all the season of snows and sins;
The days dividing lover and lover,
The light that loses, the night that wins;
And time remembered is grief forgotten,
And frosts are slain and flowers begotten,
And in green underwood and cover
Blossom by blossom the spring begins.
**Algernon Charles Swinburne**

Photography: *Joel Strasser*

Captions: *Jack Townsend*

Seasons text: *Terry Woster*

Type: *Terrie Miesen, Jan Houck*

Printed in Hong Kong by Everbest Printing Co. Ltd.